Take a Shot at Your Dreams

Before Murphy's Law Takes a Shot at You

Jamaal Saunders

786 - 942 - 1911

For my mother, who gave me her best so that I could do my best.

Contents

Wrong Place Right Time…………………….....................1

Perfect Imperfection………………………………………….24

Perish or Flourish………………………………………..48

Greatness Starts With Gratefulness…………………62

Fearlessness…………………………………………………..74

Passion Fuels Purpose…………………………………..89

Wrong Place Right Time

I always thought the words fate and destiny were just another set of cliché words reserved for those who believe in their power in shaping lives. Is it really possible to be in the wrong place at the right time? Is it possible that a mishap can inadvertently create a miracle? That destruction can lead to destiny? What if the worst moments of your life were not so at all? It is so easy to say that bad things happen to good people (another cliché in the books). Those words roll off the tongue like morning dew on mint leaves. Instead, why not say that good people happen to bad things? Being in the wrong place at the right time simply reverts back to the fact that within every mess is not only a message, but a messenger. The unfolding of purpose is not as perfect as we might make it out to be. It requires toil, time and the big test. The big test is that moment in time where we choose to either fail or prevail, to engage in flight or to fight.

Being in the wrong place doesn't mean you're in the wrong situation. It means you are in the best situation to shine. It's almost like a beam of light in a dark room. We should appreciate every problem, for success lies in problem solving. It is through solving our own pain that we are able to soothe another's. Opportunity does not care for the right place but is biased when it comes to the right time. It has a habit to show up in the wrong place most of the time. Most will say no when opportunity comes knocking because their environment does not match their desired outcome. They feel to be in the wrong place at the wrong time.

Let's reflect for a sec: When I got shot in the eye, I was in the wrong place at the right time. If it were the wrong time then I wouldn't be alive today.

What does it mean to be alive for you? This is a question that needs to be asked on a daily basis, with an answer that needs to be updated on a daily basis.

Taking a shot at your dreams is simply identifying what place you are, at what given time and then evaluating the current situation to identify the opportunity at hand. Once you identify that there *is* an opportunity, then it's your decision to say yes or no within that given time, the right time.

Bear in mind that you can make the right decisions at the wrong time, yet it is imperative that you make the right decisions at the right time. Our decisions are directly related to our dreams and goals, for every decision we make sum up to our future. We can carve and create our own future by making daily disciplined decisions. One of the most effective decision making strategies is keeping an eye on your goal.

Now let's reflect for sec: How the heck can I keep my eyes on my goals when I only have one? If I can do it with one, you can do it with two.

Establishment of your decision is a key step in decision making. When making a decision in the wrong place, you need to garner the right information so that you can weigh your options. Gathering information requires both inner and outer activity. Look within yourself and do full assessment. Also look externally, this may involve information from the internet, books or other individuals.

As you garner information, you will most likely come across multiple options to choose from. Get all the best possible options down on paper. After weighing your options you need to consider the consequences or benefits. Ensure that the evaluation of your decision is toward a righteous cause. If it is towards a righteous cause, then the universe will take over and make that moment a perfect time in the wrong place.

Another important part of decision making is to choose. Choice involves preparation. Sort out what you prefer so that you can make the best decision for yourself. Amongst the alternatives, which one seems to be the best decision for you? Which will provide the best outcome? Will it be a decision you will be proud of?

The most important part of decision making is taking action. Take action in the right direction by implementing your chosen option. Be sure to do an analysis of your decision and its effects. Most importantly be sure to follow through. Again this takes discipline. Discipline is all about control, self-control.

Temptations will be evident, however it is your responsibility to avoid and remove them. Anything that will hinder you from taking a shot at your dreams should remain out of sight and essentially out of mind. Allow only positive messages into your mind.

The mind is like a factory, it collects, stores and processes information. Whatever we allow in is what will be poured out. Focus on changing your mindset and your entire life will follow the lead. By listening to motivational and inspirational messages you will find an increase in your confidence. This improvement in confidence will erase all sense of unworthiness, doubt and fear. Then your mind will be ready and armed to face those dream-killing fears. This is how you become fearless.

Being fearless means being bold. It means letting go of what other people think and letting go of the fear of failing. Fearlessness means disregarding your status, knowing that it does not define your worth. Stay open to changes and embrace the possibilities. Do not become too attached to your plans and have an overall mission for your life. Also, don't be afraid to seek support when you need it.

Your circle of influence is a determinant factor of your discipline and ultimately your success. If all of your friends are void of self-discipline, you will have a fight sustaining it as well. There is an age old saying which goes, "show me your friends and I will tell you who you are". If self-discipline is your aim, seek friends who are enthusiastic, goal-driven and about seeing results. Being a part of a mastermind group is a very effective way to find like-minded individuals. You will be able to learn first-hand what mistakes to avoid, what roadblocks are encountered and how to move forward.

Keeping discipline at the forefront means never waiting for it to "feel right". The right time is in the present, in the now. Determine how much you want to fulfill your goal. It fuels discipline. Can you picture yourself being disciplined enough to carry out the necessary steps to reach your goals?

Visualization is highly effective in painting a near perfect, if not perfect picture in order for you to take that shot at your dreams. There is great power in visualization. What you visualize will soon be your reality. You become what you think about the most. You attain what you think about the most. Whatever you desire, think of it as if it is already yours.

Taking on your dreams might seem like a huge feet however, breaking them down into smaller action steps will make them more attainable. Also, ask a friend to keep you accountable. An accountability partner should serve as a reminder as to why you got started in the first place. Having someone to keep you accountable heightens your passion and productivity.

Take action. Get in the habit of taking daily steps toward your goals. Discipline requires daily action. This means engaging in a particular action step whether or not you feel like it. This is how you master self-discipline.

In order to form such a new habit as will be formed by your discipline, commit to at least thirty days. To get a habit to work itself, all it takes is 21 to 30 days. This is where you are conditioning the mind to work the way you want it to work. Make it through this period and you are well on your way to solidifying that habit.

Be consistent. This means daily action. Activities you do daily are the ones that form habits. Once or twice a week is not enough time to condition the mind to a habit. Keep it simple. Remember, Rome was not built in one day, therefore you cannot totally transform your life in a single day. Taking on too much initially can be overwhelming in the long run. If you ever want to take an hour out of each day to exercise, first make it a habit to work out for 15 or 20 minutes a day, then gradually increase your workout time overtime.

Set reminders to carry out your habit each day. Missing days can dilute the effectiveness of the habit. The importance of remaining consistent cannot be stressed enough. Set a schedule and stick to it. To establish a habit, we often have to give up something. Replacing that which was once a need with a new habit requires mindful substitution. If you get stress relief from eating ice cream, you might want to try exercising.

Perfection and progress are not a good mix. Immediate success in changing your habits should not be expected. Always do your very best knowing that you will have hiccups along the way. Be mindful of all negating thoughts that come to mind and find something positive replace them. Find people who represent the habits you wish to have and spend time with them. Follow and mirror their actions.

Write your goal down. Getting it down in details will make it more attainable. Knowing that you are doing it for yourself will motivate you to see your goals through. All it takes is timing and the right time.

Which takes me to time value. Time value is an important aspect of life. Enjoy every moment of your life. Happiness should not be a futuristic goal. It's a feeling you choose whether or not to have in the present. We cannot escape the passing of time. We can choose to enjoy it, however. Better understanding of time value means that we can develop an appreciation of our personal time and respect for that of others. All things done on time, will see results on time and at the right time. Only 24 hours is given to each of us in a day. We cannot live it for another, neither can another live it for us.

Time management is the foundation of a healthy life. There are several ways to approach and adjust time and the management of it. Yet, if you don't realize, let alone understand the importance of time management, approaching the matter would be a waste of time. Understanding why will be the basis of your motivation.

One reason is that time is limited. As stated earlier, there are only 24 hours in a day. That applies to you and the individual who is making a waste of their life. It also applies to that person who is where you desire to be, that person who actually took a shot at their dreams and worked ten times harder than the average dream builder. If you wish to make your dreams a reality, you have to embrace the importance of time and time management. You will begin to work smarter not harder.

Focus is heightened when you learn to maneuver your time the right way. With an increase in your ability to focus comes increased productivity. Completing tasks will be easier and faster. Can you imagine how much more time you will have on your hands by handling your time with the utmost care? People who appreciate their tome do not dare waste it by being mediocre. These individuals go above and beyond in all areas of their lives.

Refined decision-making is another benefit of proper time management. Rather than feeling short on time, with a time management technique set in place, you will experience less pressure when it comes to making decisions that need to be thought out. A lack of time often leads to quick and poor decision making. Time management allows you to carefully weigh out your options to make a fully calculated decision.

It's not new that success and time management go hand in hand. Taking a shot at your dreams and being prepared at the right time requires organization of your time. Rather than conforming to the norm of others, you will be able to take full control of your life. As you become more prompt, people around you will begin to notice and look to you to get the job done, especially in the workplace.

Being able to take advantage of opportunities is yet another perk of time management. Opportunities can pass you by if you do not have the time to see them, let alone take them up. Great time management can eliminate such a dilemma.

We all know how overwhelming it can be to not have a grasp of our time. We can become easily stressed for the sake of not having that well needed control over our time. Yet we need not succumb to such stress if we regain and maintain that control. Imagine having an important errand to run just before you head in to work and you only have half an hour to spare. What if you end up oversleeping with only enough time for you to go straight in to work? Not only would time management prevent such a mishap but the stress that would accompany it as well.

Perhaps one of the best things about time management is that it helps us to make room for recreational time. Everyone needs that special time to loosen up. Yet between all our daily activities and responsibilities it can be hard to find such free time. You can find that time by implementing management of your time. You'll be able to allocate a specific time of the day to your relaxation.

Time Management like all methods to success, requires discipline. There is no place for delay when you practice good time management. When you are disciplined with your time, you will find that it ramifies into other areas of life.

Time management is a skill that everyone aiming take a shot at their dreams should have. There are several techniques that are effective in strengthening such a skill. One of such is to create a to-do-list. Having a number of task can seem immense but by creating a to-do-list you will have the ease of time and the pleasure of checking tasks off.

Scheduling your day is another crucial time management strategy. You want to end your day before you begin it. Meaning, you want to plan out your entire day on paper ahead of time. First thing in the morning works best. Also there are lots of apps that aid in time management. It's an excellent idea to use a calendar app to log all of your appointments. You'll find that most successful individuals use a calendar. You'll see an increase in your productivity.

Taking rests in between a specific chunk of time is an effective way to capitalize on your time management. There is a technique called "The Pomodoro Technique," created by Francesco Carillon and works like this: 25 minutes work, then a 3-5 minutes break, done four times. Having those breaks in between feeds productivity especially when it settles at a certain level.

As the saying goes, "The early bird gets the most worm." It's no wonder that getting up earlier will help you to get things done on time, sometimes with time to spare. You may have a tendency to procrastinate and that creates stress and overwhelm. It's such a great feeling to wake up earlier and get high priority tasks out of the way. Exercising, believe or not powers productivity. The more productive you are is the more you get done and the more you can get done is the more control you can have on your time.

Keep room in your calendar for unexpected emergencies, events and favors friends or family member might ask of you. Though it is not healthy to yes to every single request, you do want to keep your options open. A weekly review of the week is yet another time management habit you want to develop. Organization of your work space comes first. Then prioritize your projects, tasks and activities for the week. Get up to date and remove anything on your schedule that is not a necessity. You might want to also add projects that you've been putting on the back burner. This will help you to maintain your control.

Wasted time often gets us discouraged. Don't let half an hour on the phone with your mom make you feel as though you have failed in proper management of your time. A small interruption should not make you feel guilty for lack of productivity. Simple hop back on the wagon.

Eliminate procrastination.
Whatever task you've been avoiding
should be put to the forefront so
that you can get it out the way and
thus regain the momentum of your
productivity. Take five minutes in
advance to determine your desired
result for the task at hand. What is
your desired outcome? Also take five
minutes after you have completed
the task to see if you accomplished
such an outcome. If you are not
successful, where did you go wrong?
What can you do differently?

Multitasking is a "skill" so many
pride themselves in having. Yet,
multitasking is detrimental to
productivity and consequently
success. Attack a single task at a
time. Each task deserves your full
attention and will only be
successfully completed if
approached on a one on one basis.

Get easier tasks out of the way. A small win can do wonders for your entire day. It conditions your brain into getting things done. Make your space one that is decluttered and organized. Disorganization often fuels procrastination and sometimes even causes you to never get the tasks done. Everything should have its own place and be put back in its place once you're through using them. Decluttering equals distressing.

We all have a time of the day when we are most productive. Find out what time of the day that is for you and be as productive as possible during that time. This is your time of peak performance, taking advantage of that period will have you checking things off your to-do-list.

Take a moment to pause during your day. Take a coffee or a tea break. Be sure to set aside time to eat your meals and have snacks in between. Pauses throughout your day gives you a chance to clear your mind and a well-needed boost in your productivity.

In executing proper time management, boundaries should be put in place. That means work time is work time and free time is free time. Do not allow others to interrupt your work flow, whether they be a friend or family member. Also the time you have set aside for yourself to relax should not be interrupted by clients. Do not be afraid to decline unexpected requests.

Do work in batches. A specific day should be assigned specific tasks. Switching from one task to the next can be tiresome and frustrating. Scheduling your work in batches however, allows the processes to be done with little effort.

Have a deadline in place for each of your tasks or goals. This will not only help you keep your eyes on the goal but also fuel your drive in reaching that goal. It starves procrastination. Outsourcing work can help your productivity tremendously. You cannot do it all. Outsource time-consuming tasks to another so that you can use your time for something else.

You want end your day on a great note. Instead of focusing what you did wrong or what went wrong, go to bed thinking of your day's successes. This will turnover into the following day.

Being in the wrong place at the right time does require preparation. You must be ready for that moment when opportunity will come your way. Mastering your time makes the transition of your dreams into reality a whole lot easier.

Perfect Imperfection

A perfect imperfection is that moment in time where that which was made to destroy you, only destroys your fear and drives you toward your destiny. This is where your faith in yourself and even more so in Him whom is greater than you is strengthened. You'll probably never experience something as drastic as myself yet that does not dismiss you from making the necessary steps to move from fear to faith.

Stepping out in faith is a bold step. Many fail to take advantage of the opportunities that come their way because of their lack of boldness and trust. You must believe in yourself and your abilities. God intends for us to live a life of prosperity and hope. He does His part in giving us a special desire linked to our destiny, we have to do our part by taking action. This action often requires a leap of faith.

Taking that leap doesn't mean that you won't experience challenges along the way. What's more important that these challenges is overcoming them. For one, you have to move with positive thinkers. If you're surrounded by people who practice positive thinking, when obstacles come your way, you will be more apt to seeing your goals through for the achievement of your dream. Negative individuals will have the opposite effect on you. Your focus and drive can be easily tainted by those of a negative influence. Your circle of influence will determine your own influence on your dreams.

Always remember why you got started in the first place. Why did you decide to take a shot at your dreams? Revisit the goals you have down on paper, it will give you enough motivation to take on any road block.

Keep yourself in motion. Quitting should be out of the question. Breakthrough comes to those who are persistent. The trick is to keep trying no matter what. Change your way of thinking. The thoughts you carry can either build or break your dreams. To experience success, first reconstruct your thoughts. Strong, positive thoughts equal an unbreakable sense of resilience.

Change the way you view challenges and obstacles. Challenges should be perceived as growth factors - a way to build and go beyond what might be expected of you. Don't be afraid to think big. The bigger the dream the mightier the challenge. Yet with will and willpower that challenge will be dwarfed and knocked out of the way. Do smart work not hard work. There is a misconception that hard work leads to success yet, the hardest of workers such as plumbers and carpenters tend not to be the wealthiest of individuals. Not to say the wealth equals success, yet it is a measuring tool for many.

Be your own source of motivation.
Challenges sharpen your problem
solving skills and should help you to
become the best version of yourself.
In having a mindset that does not
accept failure you can face any
challenge. Stay calm when faced
with a troubling situation. Keeping
a level head and staying collected
allows you to think things through
and make the best decision.

Allow failure to be your fuel. The
reason most shun a challenge is for
the fear of failure. Not facing a
challenge means automatic failure.
Use failures as stepping stones to
success. Each failure should be used
as a marker that you are one step
closer to hitting that bull's eye.

Just like a major goal, a challenge is
more approachable when you
simplify it. Break your challenge
down into smaller steps. As you
break through each step you garner
the confidence you need to see all
the steps through to the very final
one.

Such confidence must be maintained. The challenge must first be tackled and eliminated in the mind. Believe that you can. Analyze the different ways that you can approach the problem and work them out in your mind first before you execute each approach. Until you confirm the win in your mind you will be unable to achieve it in reality.

Focus on the best possible outcome. If you happen to not overcome a challenge, keep your spirit up. It is such failure that molds you into a more thick-skinned individual who is after their goals. You'll need that when life starts throwing the rocks again.

Perfection kills progress and you need progress in order to see that you are moving in the direction of your dreams. This is why within every deemed "imperfection" is the perfect moment of change which leads to progress.

To make progress, decide why you gradual betterment. The reasons for wanting to move forward might be many. It could that you are tired of your current position in life or that you ended up at a place you didn't expect to be.

Sometimes being passive about the route your life has taken can cause you to end up where you no longer want to be. That's your cue that it is time to make progress. First ask yourself, "Why the need for the sudden change? Does this desire come from internal or external forces?" Is the need based on your own desire or what is expected of you? Be sure that you are seeking progress to fill your new expectations and not that of society or someone else.

Be okay with your current position and current self. It might seem conflicting that you want progress yet you believe all is well but, judging yourself will not motivate you to move onward. Negative thoughts and emotions will only prevent you from making progress. Do not connect your emotions to your goal, instead feel that you are worthy for that which you want to accomplish.

Remain thoughtful during the undertaking. Progress comes with many actions that will require you to step outside of your comfort zone. It's not all smooth sailing. Upon facing the inevitability of challenges and failures, remaining thoughtful will help you to take a step back and take a look at the big picture. Being able to do this will allow you to see where you went wrong and how you can do better the next time around.

Accept the likely mishaps. In the process of progress, setbacks are natural happenings. While this does not destroy the line of progress, it can derail it. This shouldn't make you falter in faith or your belief in yourself. It's all about getting up and keeping it moving.

Celebrate your successes. This is a part of progression that is many times overlooked. As you hit milestones, celebrate! Treat yourself to something nice. Not only does this boost your confidence but it feeds your desire as well. Be sure to marinate in your victories. Once you get results, enjoy the fact that you have achieved them. We have a tendency to jump from one goal to the next rather than savoring the results of each.

A perfect imperfection correlates to the notion that everything happens for a reason. Therefore anything that seems to happen out of place is in perfect alignment to what is meant to be. Every mistake is a chance to master yourself and is a sign that it is time for improvement.

There are a plethora of ways in
which you can improve yourself.
One such way is to build upon your
skills. You do this by learning from
your own experience and vicariously
from the experience of others.
Waking up early greatly improves
your productivity and your way of
life. Waking up early gets you in a
pace that will be steady throughout
your day.

Get out of your comfort zone.
Change and comfort do not live in
the same place. It takes significant
work for improvement to take place.
We tend to settle when we are
comfortable. We have to expose
ourselves to new environments and
new people in order to experience
change.

Identify your weaknesses. Become
more aware of yourself and your
reaction to certain people and
situations. At times, it is our blind
spots that keep us from improving.

Learning what they are and working on them can greatly facilitate betterment. One way to do this is to ask friends, family members, co-workers or someone you are close to their perspective. What are your flaws? How can you improve them?

Learn from those who inspire you. If you wish to be successful, find someone who is doing what you desire to do and emulate them. Try to acquire the skills and qualities that they have. Quit your bad habits and form new ones that benefit you.

Not only will difficult times come your way but also difficult people. As much as you might not want to, you must learn how to deal with those individuals. On the one hand you have time management and on the other you have people management. Whether it be at home or in the workplace, you must be able to manage the people you are surrounded by.

Seek out a mentor or coach. You can reach your desired level of improvement significantly faster with a coach or mentor by your side. Having someone to work with you on clarifying and seeing your goals through will help you to see results. It also helps to network with people who are at a good rank in their field or industry. These people have become accomplished because they have the right mindsets, expertise and knowledge. They have a competence that you can gain some insight from.

The past can hinder you from focusing on your future. Holding on to the past prevents your development. It is essential that you let go of the past and carry on. Also, be kind to those around you. Kindness should be given freely. When we are kind we begin to engage in other acts of love. Not only will you make another feel great but yourself as well.

Commit to your improvement. It takes a personal commitment to embrace change and the whole process behind it - the good, the bad and all the perfect imperfections.

If you are truly committed to living the life of your dreams you first have to get your mindset right. All faucets of success require a strong unwavering mind. Nothing can derail the mind and have you going of course more than a mind filled with broken beliefs and presumptions. Come to a solid decision of not allowing anything to come in between you and your success. Take inventory of your life and dedicate yourself to taking a powerful shot at your dreams.

Fine-tune your goals. Make your goals very specific. Get crystal clear on your desired outcome. Know what you want, how you will achieve it and in what period of time. Your vision should be so big that nothing will hinder you from reaching.

It is time to put that list of goals to action, and if you don't have a list, then now is a good time to start. Setting goals is the first step toward reaching success, but even more important is acting towards those goals.

You must find the drive to do all which is necessary to help you reach where you are destined to be. Each small act is still considered progress. If you need to take small steps, then do so, so long as you are walking in the direction of your goals. I urge you however, not to take too many small steps for long, as time is at hand.

You need to secure each goal promptly, so set reasonable deadlines. Always have your list of goals at hand, you must be constantly reminded of what you are working for and towards. Goals, when attained, become contributors to a better, more valuable you. Adding value attracts value. So then, if you become more valuable, then you will attract success in its plethora of variations. Success and value go hand in hand, you cannot have one without the other. Become goal-oriented. It's a trait that shines in all successful individuals. If you want what an accomplished man has, do what he does.

Make what's important your focal point. With the hustles and bustles of life, and all the responsibilities in between, it can be difficult to pinpoint what the main priorities are. Your own personal freedom is the ultimate goal. Therefore, how you allocate your time is crucial.

Hold yourself responsible. While motivation is needed to get you started, accountability is needed for you to stay committed to your dreams. Follow through on your weekly and daily goals. Don't be afraid to share your goals and ambitions with others, even unsupportive friends and family members. Making your dream public will help you stay committed. Become a part of a group or community so that you can be around people who share similar goals. These individuals will be encouraging and expecting your success. This will give you the self-assurance and drive to commit.

A perfect imperfection ramifies into the purpose behind the pain. Every downfall is cushioned by your purpose. If you've ever feel lost or as though something is missing, it might be that you need that perfect imperfection. With every error in judgement comes perfection of judgement and with every mistake comes the clarification of knowing what to do. Therefore all things are right and in alignment with the fulfilling of your purpose. Everything happens in your favor according to your faith.

Finding our purpose requires action, thinking alone won't do. Finding your purpose and living out your passions require a whole lot of doing. Overthinking cost many people their purpose. Many of us are afraid of the unknown and therefore we never dare to jump into new things. Take action steps in the direction of your dreams. Most times nothing is in our way but our own selves. Get out of the way and get into action. With more action comes more clarity.

Get out of your head and into your heart. Sometimes it takes that perfect imperfection to propel you into doing what you truly love to do. Know where your heart is and allow it to lead you to your purpose and passion. The heart is inspired while the head is wired. It's such a great feeling to not only be inspired but do what inspires you.

There is a common misconception that we are all meant to do only one thing. Not only does that limit our purpose but it can cause a lot of inner turmoil as well. Detach yourself from that number one. The more things you delve into is the sooner you will realize your full potential. Find out all you can do and do as many of the things you find out. Live a life of passion, it that which will power your purpose.

I speak a lot about finding a community but it is just as important to build a community of your own. If you cannot find an already standing group of individuals who are for a similar cause, then create one of your own. In fact, you can do both.

Sharing your story is a sure way to groom and grow your purpose. The process of encountering and overcoming depicts development. You'll find that others will relate to your story and you may very well be helping many of whom might feel trapped in a circumstance you overcame.

Sometimes all the arrows might be pointing in one direction, yet you get that one feeling outside of those pointers called a "gut feeling". It's a perfect imperfection also called your instinct. You don't have to understand why you are having that particular feeling which is seeming to go against something that you desire, however you must know that it's there and you must acknowledge it.

Many people tend to confuse their initial thought as instinct, or even fear, anxiety and other resisting forces. Instincts are not activated in apparent danger but rather in decision making. It not a reflex so much as it's a reasoning.

We tend to look to our instincts to avoid or approach a troubling question we have crafted in our heads. You might think that following your instincts might have left you empty handed but in fact, it has taken you to exactly where you need to be. Not where you necessarily want to be but where you need to be.

On the other opposite side of resistance is your instinct. Where there is turmoil so too is a resisting force. Your instinct is on the other side of fear. If you are afraid of taking a shot at your dreams then what you instinctively want is for your dream to become a reality.

Your instinct isn't always a whirlwind of emotions but rather an indistinct signal or subconscious reaction. A lot of time your instinct presents itself through a subtle change in the way you feel or a small spark of awareness.

To be aware of that gut feeling, the
mind must be settled. To completely
understand what your instinct is
trying to tell you your mind must be
in a non-analyzing state. Instincts
tend to occur in the whim of the
moment.

Hearing your instincts is not as
important as trusting your instincts.
It's one thing to desperately search
for what your instinct is saying and
whole other to hear it loud and
clear, but not want to accept what
you hear. Your instincts will not
always pin a direct line from you to
what you want, but it will most
certainly steer you to what you
need.

To trust your instincts do follow
your interest. Instincts tend to nag
until there are carried out in action.
It is that instinct which drives the
urge to move in a specific direction.
You must commit yourself to your
instinctual action. That hunch you
have must be upheld by fearless
work and dedication.

Submerge yourself in all that which has to do with your pursuit. Your industry of interest will require not only innate instincts but instincts based upon experiences as well. The more you learn, the more you will be able to make quick instinctual choices stemmed from your knowledge.

Disregard the rules. Old rules are for old instincts. It takes a true leader to follow his own gut and generate new directives. When you don't conform to the norm the chances of failure is high, however instincts will tell you what to fix and what to do better the next time around. Then, the chances of success will be high because you are constantly refining your dream.

Allow your dream to change, to expand and to be perfected. Your instinct should allow flexibility, for as you develop so too should your dream. Giving yourself the freedom of change will aid you in having confidence in your instincts.

As stated throughout, trust is a key part of following through with your instincts. One way to build self-trust to stay away from negative individuals who get a thrill out of seeing you fail. You have total control over the people you allow into your life. Be sure to keep promises to yourself. What commitments you make to yourself, you get to keep. Not only will you build trust but your sense of dedication as well.

Be kind to yourself. Why say certain things to ourselves that we wouldn't dare say to another? The voices on the shoulder and in the head can be pretty loud. You can silence them by being a bit more understanding toward yourself.

Remember, a good relationship with yourself ramifies into your other relationships. Self-trust is about managing your mistakes rather than feeling you need to get everything right.

It's about experiencing failure and not becoming too flustered but rather fascinated at how it will help you in the future. Self-trust is not about perfection. As a matter of fact it comes with ton of perfect imperfections.

For whatever course or field you chose to make your endeavor, application of strict regimens should be noted and acted out. Every single day, movement should be made toward your desires. You'll find that the path becomes more lighted, and easier to travel on. A lifestyle of your choosing is what you are creating.

Taking small yet continuous steps will eventually enable you to become a confident claimer. Your desires, dreams and goals are already yours. However, you must practice claiming it through action steps toward those ends. This is so that once you reach your destination you will be who you hoped to be. The perfect time will never come for you to initiate your destiny.

Life is naught but a big test. In order to pass, plant persistence in your entire being. Life is also a cycle, one to be broken. That takes courage, probably the most you will ever need. Yet, that frightening step will set you free. That frightening step will remove those inner shackles you have placed on yourself. Forget fear and fight for freedom by training yourself to be your future self. Remember, you are who you hope to be.

Perish or Flourish

The difference in the decision to sink or survive is in your power. All of us have a strong inner power but not all of us know how to unlock it.

The mystery that we call life perhaps may never be fully solved. There is but the trail left by others and the gift of instinct to depend on as guides. That the thing which scares us the most and holds us down the most, when faced, provides lifelong liberation, is ironic.

You would be surprised what a man can become when he is in a position of do or die, of the power he is capable of unleashing, of the greatness he's willing to believe in. When I was on my hospital bed crippled by pain, that's a decision I had to make.

Some need a taste of how bad things can get before they feel the need to launch themselves into something better. The climb to the top starts at the bottom, and the race to the finish line begins at the start line. It is not unusual to start at nothing to amount to something. Don't feel sorry for yourself, feel proud for choosing to be strong through the storm.

Physical exercise is important and so too is mental exercise. Yet so many neglect mental fitness, which is needed to fuel power. One way to work the mind and unleash your power is to meditate. Meditation engages the mind in relaxation and promotes a good flow of energy. It helps with stress and facilitates peace. With such tranquility and ease of stress you can come to a state of joy. This will assist you in unleashing your inner power. Meditation also helps to convert negative thinking into positive thinking. A calm and clutter-free mind is needed to unlock that inner power.

Realize that you are more than just flesh and blood. You are more than just your physical self. Don't fail to recognize that your true nature is associated with your mind and spirit. If you do fail, you will not get to realize your potential power. Your body is merely a container to the mind and spirit. While the body is limited, the mind is limitless in its power and capabilities.

Thoughts are things and whatever we think, we attract. Whatever we think, we become. The law of attraction governs our daily experiences. It gives to those who ask and truly believe it will be given. Pay keen attention to your feelings. Your feelings have a lot to do with what you're currently experiencing in your life. Where you are is where you have thought yourself up to be. If there is something you desire to change, you first have to change your thoughts. Mastery of the law of attraction is a must if you wish to unlock your power.

How much do you believe in
yourself? Your self-esteem plays a
role in the magnitude of your power.
Make note of your accomplishments
and improve your capabilities. Get
to know yourself and you will come
to find that you have more power
than you know. Be confident in your
ability that you can take a solid shot
at your dreams and continuously
feed your mind with positive
thoughts.

Identify your gifts. Everyone has a
gift whether hidden or needing
discovery. These gifts need to be put
to use and shared with the world.
Use your gifts wisely and hold
yourself responsible for road you are
led to take because of your actions,
whether good or bad. Failure to
recognize your gifts is failure to give
yourself permission to unleash your
power.

You possess the ability to save
yourself. God has given to each of
us, a unique skill or ability, a talent
which is not meant to be hidden. It
is a part of your destined greatness.
Show it to the world! It is a part of
who you are.

Do not deem it unworthy to be the vessel which transports you to your desired lifestyle. You have to give of yourself in order to get for yourself. What do you have to offer to success? Success requires payment to receive its services. Payment which must be given in advance. The good part is, success only requires discipline in developing and showcasing your talent and ideas

So lack of money and a college education in this instance, would be excuses. The worst thing you could possibly do is excuse yourself from your dreams. Examine yourself and find what you can give. If not a talent or skill, then an idea will do. It is not effective to merely think but to act immediately despite the look of your bank account and your level of education.

Believe in yourself, you are God's tool, and every tool serves a purpose. You have meaning and purpose. There is a role you must fulfil or you will have died to leave nothing for the world.

Instead of being influenced by all the negativity you face each day, choose to be a person of influence. Face the challenges you are surrounded by and be the light in the midst of the dark. This is how you unlock your potential power and turn it into applied power. Control of yourself no matter the circumstance is where true power lies.

Know that if you are going forward there will always be a force or forces pulling you back. You are in a constant tug of war between reaching your goals and simply never reaching them. It is you at one end, and fear, doubt, indecisiveness, demotivation, and oppression at the other end. You are going against a monster team.

So you see then that you have to hold tight to the rope and tread onwards? It requires strength. It requires fearlessness and certainty, quick yet efficient decision making and motivation, and ultimately freedom. Study the characteristics of these forces so that you can quickly repel them. These fatalistic forces do not reveal themselves upfront. Not one will announce their intent to visit you. They all wear a façade, masquerading in the masks of banal matters, or a job, or a parent, or a boss, or a spouse. Which makes it difficult to address or even shun them.

Realize that the mind is the target. Do not mind the physicality of these forces, that's not the way to fight and defend yourself. There is but one way to arm yourself, and that is through consistency of efforts and immediate disposal of those forces upon their birth.

Choosing whether or not to perish or flourish is comes down to your motivation. You are either positively motivated from thinking of all the good things that will happen as a result of your actions, or negatively motivated from thinking of all the bad things that will happen. While both are effective depending on the circumstance, positive motivation will propel you further in the direction you wish to go.

To become motivated, set goals. Goals give you a specific direction to go. Goals are a measure of your success. Whether or not you achieve them will indicate whether or not you need to try again or that you have succeeded. Work towards things that you actually enjoy doing. Choose goals that peak your interest. Do what's best for you rather than what's expected of you.

Plot your progress. Seeing how far you've come in accomplishing your goals can increase motivation. Having a map or visual representation is a great way to track your progress.

Motivation should not be wished for, it should be worked for. What is your aim? What is the end result? What reason do you have for pressing on? When you find these, if you haven't already, then giving up will not be an option. Lay the foundation - put in the work, so that building your house – designing your future, will be met with passion and vigor.

Each time you feel unsure, or afraid, or dubious, summon your reasons and they should save you. They should, if they are good enough reasons. Be strong even when weakness and pain cripple you. Some of the most powerful ideas and creations come only with pain.

Pain, though a feeling to be shunned, is indication of future triumph. Embrace pain as the foreshadowing of better things to come. Excuses are so easy to use. Trash them. Delete them from your mind. They are limitations. If your pursuits mean anything to you, then excuses will mean nothing. Excuses are reasons against your reasons, rebuttals to your progression. Delete them from your mind.

Becoming a master of manifestation can help you to flourish in all areas of your life. The foundation of manifestation is gratitude. Your world mirrors your attitude. Having gratitude shows appreciation for the things that are already present in your life. In showing such appreciation you're manifesting more of what you desire.

Ask for divine intervention. Let go of trying to fix everything yourself and surrender all control to God. Seek His guidance and ask for direction.

Act as though you are already living your dreams. Visualize your future in detail. What do you see, smell, feel, hear and taste? Make preparations for your dreams to arrive. If you wish to be financially free for example, do you have a savings account in place? Do you have an investment plan? Have you set up a budget?

Don't become attached to a specific outcome. Keep an open mind, opportunities often came in unexpected, even unwanted ways. Trust that your dreams will bloom.

Again, trust your intuition. Follow that hunch you've been feeling. Your instincts will guide you into taking the right actions. Do not attach your happiness to your future. Practice being happy presently with the life you have now. Manifestation is closely linked to how you are feeling now. It is essential that you live in the present moment. Placing your focus on then pains of the past or the worries of the future will only cause you to be blind to all the blessings around you. You will not be able to see what you ought to be grateful for.

Throw away the deadweight of worrying. Worrying is the equivalent of wasting your time. Instead put all your efforts into productive activities. How many occasions have you worried over something only to find out it wasn't necessary? That's it, it is just not necessary. How will worrying help you? It doesn't. The future holds so many surprises, do not worry yourself of what life has wrapped up for you. Instead, design and create what you want from life and make that your aim.

Then you won't have to concern yourself of what is in store for you. You will know what to expect. This is not to say that the future is predictable but rather moldable. You can achieve exactly what you want out of this life. Simply focus your time and energy on the plan you have created.

If the ball does not enter the goal, it often times it brushes the net. The feelings of doubt and worry attack us all. What makes the outcome of each individual different is how they function during these emotions.

Do not tarry during the tears for it is easy to stay down, when down. However, if you have a moment of weakness, gather up all the strengths of the past and look past your current state enough to keep going. Carry on.

Each day has success behind it. Celebrate them. Sometimes we are so focused on reaching our dreams that we fail to take notice of our daily wins. Affirmations are an excellent way to prep the mind for success and happiness.

They are usually "I am" statements that empower and strengthen the mind. For example: I am strong. I am powerful. I am enough. In saying affirmations you must do so with feeling and belief. Again, manifestation works when you feel and believe.

Greatness Starts With Gratefulness

Until you appreciate what you already have, you won't be able to appreciate better when it comes your way. Do not carry the problems of yesterday into your new day. That will only hinder your productivity. It is right to desire more or better, but not at the cost of your happiness. Not having what you desire should not trigger sadness within, but motivation. Let your downfalls drive you to your destiny. Be grateful for all you have, for many are penniless and alone.

Riches come in many forms, so do not chase the dollars, chase the dreams, which is where your fortune lies. You might have a family that the wealthy man wishes to have, or be in better health, or have a better personality and vice versa.

There is a man out there with a vision outlaid on paper, who is going head on for what he wants knowing that success, though not immediate, is inevitable with work. You must desire to have what he has - an insatiable hunger for success, and not the money of the millionaire. After all, the mind must match the money or one will surely be lost. Groom yourself for success or success won't stay for long.

In order to make gratitude a daily habit, get down on paper what you are grateful for. Keep a journal and write in it daily. Jot down at least ten things you are grateful for.

Practice being in the moment. "I'm busy" is the ruling excuse of the day. It is so easy to get caught away with daily routine that little memories and moments are missed. So caught away with tomorrow or next week or next month that today is forgotten and lost. So special is today that there will be no other day quite like it. Take time to focus your senses. Do you hear the cars zooming by? See the bright blue of the sky?

Feel the breeze brushing your skin?
Savor each bite that you're taking?
Or take a whiff of fresh air? Be
mindful of your surroundings. Even
more so be mindful of your loved
ones. They are your backbone.
Sometimes they are yearning for
your attention, your hugs and your
kisses. Be sure to give those
abundantly. Lastly, be mindful of
your dreams.

Many a time dreams are drowned in
the sea of schedule. Time must be
given to the planning and
undertaking of what you truly
desire or it will forever stay just
that... a desire. Appreciation of
what was dealt to you is virtue in
itself. Appreciation of the good, for it
shapes you; appreciation of the bad,
for it builds you. Do not confuse
however appreciation with
acceptance. You possess the will to
create change.

Practicing selflessness can really fuel your sense of gratefulness. Get involved in something bigger than yourself. Volunteer for a particular cause or become involved in helping others. This will help you to see that you are more fortunate than you think you are and that will bring you to a state of gratitude.

Let others know that you appreciate them. Let them know that you are thankful for what they do for you and the love they show you. In turn, show them some love. Turn in your complaints for gratitude. Instead of focusing on what you don't have search for what you can be thankful for.

Plant seeds of greatness.Whatever work you put in will be the equivalent of what you get out. Do not expect a little for a lot. It has never worked that way and never will. Do not sit and wait for something great and miraculous to happen to you, it never will. The work has to be put in. So many people are walking around in nothingness. So many people are lacking purpose because they fail to mold a path for themselves.

You are the shaper of your life. God gave us all free will, where you end up in this realm is your responsibility.

A man in the gutter shouldn't blame anyone for his position but himself. Likewise, a man in the hills shouldn't give any man praises for his greatness but himself. The second you become the owner of your actions, is the second you will realize the power you carry to turn your life around and gain control of the steering wheel. Dare to act on your dreams, dare to make an idea become a tangible object, dare to be the very best you can be – those are the seeds that will bear fruits of unimaginable greatness.

It is the compilation of the good times and the bad times, of mistakes made and lessons learnt – life. You must learn to thrive as much in the difficult moments as in the wonderful ones. Know that trials will come. Develop the skills to handle them well, if not with ease.

See these trials as lessons rather than problems, for each will make you more experienced and apt to manage future obstacles. Find strength in the valley, and build strength on the mountain top.

In other words, in the lowest of times, you must draw from the available resources within you and around you. There is a message, a guideline in every area of your life. You must go searching for them however, for they are hidden. You must be able to pinpoint them when they become visible. These messages are in the books you read, the songs and sermons you listen to, the conversations you hold, observations of others, artwork, nature, and the list could go further. On the other hand, in the highest of times, be sure to solidify your strong suits, for these will sustain you in the valley. Keep your eyes open, your mind alert, and your body strong. Dare to be great! Challenge yourself. Growth is impossible without a test of abilities.

Settling at your current level takes you further away from your envisioned lifestyle. In order to grow you must seek to become a better version of yourself. To become comfortable means to accept the lie that eminence is not within you. Do not be afraid of your greater self.

You are destined to be greater than you are. Shine your light on the masses in spite of their judgements and opinions. Nothing worth having comes without a fight. The world is waiting, you have something they need, you have something to offer.

Do not let fear of failure stop you from showcasing your greatness. Do you want to live the same mediocre life for the rest of your life? So many are living just to die. They don't know that a legacy makes them live on forever. What are you going to leave behind for others to see? Since death is inevitable, then it's wise to face it head on with your dreams unfolding and your greatness being beheld. Search the depths of your heart and soul to find your truest desires, and create a plan to achieve them. It's a challenge, but isn't it worth your dreams becoming?

Ah! Such beauty lies in the moment. Why then do we focus on the worries of tomorrow, when the worries of tomorrow only steal the joy of today? The trick is to focus, capture and lock. Focus on what you are doing in the moment, and where you are. How many times have you physically been somewhere but mentally absent? So be present.

Capture, make it your possession, the smell, taste, sight, and feel of each increment of time. Lock in what you have captured, this is the creation of memories - the only things left to hold on to when the moment is gone.

Memories are collections of souvenirs of the past. Remember, though you cannot control what happens in the moment, you have total control of what you lock in. Be sure only to lock in those things which will aid in your happiness or growth.

No man knows what the future brings. It is not wise to worry of the unknown. Allow life to make its natural ebb and flow, its natural ups and downs and all-arounds.

Enjoy the flexibility of the moment rather than try to sum up the future. The present is a gift. Unwrap it and be surprised. What's life without surprises?

Do not allow mediocrity and complacency to set in. Do you know what it feels like to be extraordinary? Do you know what it feels like to live an extraordinary life? The quality of your life can be bettered through the bettering of your quality of mind. You have to want more, desire more and believe that you deserve more.

The only remedy for mediocrity and complacency is action, and action mixed with a sense of urgency. You need to keep moving. When the feeling of giving up and settling comes over you, you need to keep moving. It is so easy to become stuck in one place. So many people are stuck, with no vision for themselves, no sense of moving upwards and forward. Just keep climbing the ladder, take it a step at a time. Eventually you will reach. Refuse to be comfortable, refuse to compromise and make it your aim to conquer.

Life is so strange. Full of surprises. Full of the unexpected. How freely we roam like the breeze, only to be restricted by the pressures of life. Envision yourself to have the soul of a child, with the worries being gone forever. All children see is the moment.

The moment to have fun or cry, to shout for joy or wail in pain. The moment. Do not forget how important the present is. Being lost in the future or the past can rob you of your now, your present precious moments in life. The challenge is to remember to be present in the present, the here and now. Just stop... take a second... and breathe.

You are alive. Do you know what that means? That means you have one more shot at your dreams, one more shot to make everything right, and one more shot at the choice to be happy. Forget about everything that is happening around you and... breathe. You have life.

Be thankful. Many are rotting in their graves with their dreams right beside them. Power comes with having life.

Fearlessness

Filling your mind with the negatives will only produce negative outcomes. If you tell yourself you cannot do something, then surely you won't be able to do it. All things, great and small, good and evil, start at the mind. Master the discipline of controlling your thoughts.

Think empowering and uplifting thoughts. You are in control of your thoughts and furthermore, your actions. Great power lies with the man who does not limit himself to his immediate skills. He constantly challenges himself to be better than he is, and to do greater than he is doing. It is he that will find comfort in realizing his calling in life.

It is he that will rest in the arms of his destiny and attract his truest desires. The moment you eliminate the negatives from your vocabulary, and essentially, your mind, is the moment you will feel the motivation and the fire of inspiration to take you closer to your goals.

Avoid those who belittle your ideas and your dreams, they will only limit you. YOU NEED NO LIMITATIONS. Go for what you want head on and with full force, and if failure should meet you, then try again, for success should meet you soon enough.

Your circumstances do not define you. You hold the power to create change. Make that definite change in direction by subtracting all which is breaking you and adding all which will make you. Redefine your agenda. Do not be afraid to take risks, change entails taking risky routes.

Know that your circumstances are only temporary – the reason to put in the work and keep moving. Keep moving, it is essential that you do so or life will not hesitate to keep you down and behind. It is when you stop moving that life gets ahead of you. Stop complaining of your current station in life and make the best of it. Do your greatest at your current level, for it is a level you must pass before you can go on to the next.

It won't hurt to smile, or to have a positive attitude. As a matter of fact, your attitude is a key factor in the progress you should make. Ultimately, your attitude is a choice, it's your choice. It is your choosing to be happy or sad, vibrant or dull, enduring or weak. The future is important, but do not settle your mind so much on the future, that you forget the gift of today. There will be no other day quite like today. Live for the moment.

There is power in every thought. How strong is your mind? Do you know that you have the ability to turn your life completely around by simply changing the way you think? Imagine having control over the mishaps in your life.

If the rain falls, do not think you are going to get wet, instead think: where do I find an umbrella so I can get to where I planned on going? In the same way, when problems sneak in, do not shrink in fear of how they will affect you, instead, refine your thinking and see each problem as a piece of life's puzzle.

A piece, though complicated, that will create a full picture, that will aid in your sense of fulfilment. How you see your circumstances is all a matter of the mind. Elevate yourself from your situation and apply the skills of problem solving. Learn to work more on bettering yourself than bettering your situation, then and only then, will problems seem less like problems and more like tests to pass. These tests should be easy passes if you have become the person with the right mindset. Overturn your problems into solutions to your way out, for if they don't ruin you, then they surely build you, and a more improved you is key.

Change is often times feared. I encourage you to see change in all its beauty, it is the only thing that will provide a different direction. Do not become accustomed to the life you are living if you're not comfortable with it. God gave you free will and with that comes the power and ability to mold your destiny.

You hold the power to turn your life around, to set your sail in a different direction. You are the captain of your ship. A captain must be able to adjust his sail to any turbulence in order to keep his boat afloat. You mustn't drown, change direction if necessary, as long as the destination is your destiny. Reread the proceeding sentence, absorb its meaning. Change is not easy, but isn't it worth your happiness? It is within human nature to adapt, you will adapt to change. I press you however, to force yourself out of your situation. Do not allow yourself to adapt to a toxic environment, relationship or workplace. Block the fists of mediocrity, fight back, for it's so easy for life to keep you down if you choose to remain down. Change is not only good, but it's necessary for a better future. Change is not the enemy, complacency is. Which one do you choose?

Don't let those around you limit or hinder you with their opinions of how you should live YOUR life. A lot of times we rob ourselves of our greatness by listening to the opinions others have of our ideas or plans.

Make a decision and do not turn on it or change it, regardless of oppositions. All greatness is usually tested. Focus on your journey. Focus on the map you have drawn up for yourself. Any form of distraction will only derail you or cause a terrible accident. That halt will destroy your timing or make it inevitably longer for you to reach what waits ahead for you.

Avoid false alarms. Refrain from putting your map aside to deal with someone else's madness. Horses that pull carriages wear blinders to prevent them from becoming distracted or panicked by what is behind or beside them. A horse pulling a carriage is a horse with a destination, much different from a regular barn horse. Be like that horse pulling a carriage, forget about your past, and do not become distracted by what's around you.

Put on your mind's blinders. Straight ahead, that's where you're headed.

The best and most rewarding investment anyone can make is in themselves. Believe in yourself and dreams enough to take those big risks, to plant the necessary seeds. A reluctance to act on your ideas, dreams and desires will only forfeit the passion that is needed to drive them.

That is how the flame is outed, and so too your chances of reaching success. Invest the money, invest the effort, and most important, invest the time in you. You are the key, the main tool to the unfolding of something quite beautiful. How will you know what you have inside unless you nourish and give water, which is action, to your thirsty dreams, suffocated ideas, and dying desires? Do not hesitate. The time is now, this very moment. Do not put a hold on your future. Get the necessary tools and put them to use, it is very important that you do. For as the saying goes, anything that is not used, is surely lost.

If your dreams, ideas, and desires live inside of you, and are lost along the way, wouldn't it be safe to say that you are a lost being yourself? For who is a man without his dreams? As a bird without its wings and a ship without a sail.

Stop searching for the easy way out. It doesn't exist. Your journey will come with tears, moans, groans, sweat, and blood. It is part of the success reaching package. Nothing worthy of your time will come easy. Get the work done down to the very intricate details, that way in the future you won't suffer from having to take steps backyards.

Sometimes the shortcut ends in a dead end. A dead end means turning back and starting all over again. Now, there is nothing wrong with restarting from point A, but everything wrong with knowing it could be avoided. Think of life as a circle. Full and round, with so much to offer. Imagine cutting straight across, only to reach the end of your life not experiencing its curves.

The journey is longer going all the way around but far more intriguing and exciting and fulfilling. Focus on the journey and the ride won't seem so long. At the end of it all, you will be dipped in so much experience, both good and bad, that you will turn an expert on life. Suddenly, at the end of it all, life won't seem so difficult. Suddenly, you will have reached exactly where you dreamed of being. Isn't that beautiful?

Face your fears. Fear breeds but one thing... pain. Living in the shadow of your fears creates more damage than to take a risk and fail. What has you trembling? What has you so scared that your heart seems to skip a beat, your chest seems to tighten? You probably haven't deciphered the locks that have been placed on each stage of life.

For them to open means you have to come face to face with that which you are afraid of. It is a stage to overcome or a stage to remain, with a bright future beyond those closed doors.

You probably haven't realized that with the last of those locks is paired that which you fear the most, that there is, finally, a breakthrough when you break through that goliath of a fear that has you shrinking every time you make progress. Demolish your demons. It is what you must do or remain forever in a cycle of nothingness. Yes, if you take a look at the extremes, those are your choices, emptiness or fulfilment, nothingness or Destiny. It is time for you to make your move. Make your gambit.

You might be the source of your own failure. It is a truth many come to grip with, often when it's too late. Evaluate yourself. In what ways are you causing damage to your dreams through your actions? The man yearning for change is not fixed in his ways but rather open to change for the reason of growth. Dreams are kept alive through discipline. If you decide to rid yourself of a self-destructive habit, and you should, then do not line yourself up for failure.

That is the man who plans on waking up earlier than usual yet doesn't set his alarm, or decides he wants to lose weight yet still eats a burger and drinks soda every day. What are you willing to sacrifice for your personal growth? What negative inclinations are you willing to erase from your personality? Know your weak areas and work to either eliminate what's unnecessary or strengthen what is needed.

Only you can accurately pinpoint those things which are slowly clipping your wings, making you unable to soar to greater heights. Before attempting to spread your wings and fly, ensure those wings are not tied to your body. That would be a set up for disaster and that's not your aim.

Strength is the ability to have moments of weakness and not let them affect your course of action. If you can fall on your knees and still reach the finish line, then that is strength. Strength is being able to say "My failures do not define me; instead they guide me to my true path."

It's a matter of the mind as much as it is a matter of the physical, if not more so. What will be said of the man who in his weakest moment reaches his threshold? Or of the man who manages to make a fortune with an empty pocket but so much in his head? Strength and action will remedy the cuts and bruises of failure. Failure is only permanent if you choose for it to be so.

Do not allow yourself to drown when you are down. Get up with urgency; see the failure as temporary and move on to the next plan or route. Trial and error go hand in hand, but not forever. You can try and fail for only so long. There will arrive a point when you have tried and succeeded. That makes all the trials even more approachable. Success is inevitable, if only you don't quit and remain strong.

Delete Doubt. Nothing stirs the human mind quite like doubt. It is enough to dry the well of inspiration and motivation, and gives fear a way to sneak in. Surety and fearlessness are in the heart of the success-seeker. Doubt is a wild animal with you as its target.

Tame this beast with immediate action. So many are the reasons why you cannot, yet it may take just one sound reason to propel you to the stars. Do not focus on the negatives. Get rid of the "what ifs". There is no better way to solve the unknown, than to test it. Keep testing until the odds are in your favor, for each failure means one step closer to success.

Believe in yourself and your capabilities. Believe that within you is the secret to success. Within you is the antidote for mediocrity. Do not doubt your power. Say "I can and I will." Repeat it if you must. Shout it out if you must, "I can and I will." I CAN AND I WILL. It's called willpower, the mixture of your power and your willingness to use it. As that old saying goes, "Where there is a will, there is a way." So if you can only see it and believe it, then you can reach it and achieve it.

Passion Fuels Purpose

Have pride in your passion. Why are so many talents described as hidden? Why are so many afraid to talk about their dreams? Murmuring instead of speaking boldly of what they love? Your passion can make you profits and profits can do so much more than ordinary wages.

With your passion in mind, you can work for yourself and in the direction of *your* dreams rather than someone else's. Your passion provides a promise to you that your path will be lightened and lighted. The joy of following your passion is that the pain becomes worth it.

The work becomes worthy of your time even if you are not being paid right away for it. A great majority will agree that they dread their regular job. It doesn't matter if they are being paid nine dollars or ninety dollars for the hour. When your time is sold for the main benefit of someone else, how can you ever expect to be happy?

It's an appropriation of a large portion of your day, and consequently your life to lockdown. Imprisonment of oneself and one's dreams. It is a mindless act that many submit themselves to every single day, praying that everything will suddenly be alright. Nothing will ever be alright until you fix yourself and your mind. Embrace your passion and then sell it.

Being a part of society often leads to the conformation to what everyone else is doing. Those who dare to travel their own path suffer criticism and misunderstanding. Yet still, they are the ones who end up being leading innovators, successful business men and women, and free from the suppressive system that has been set up.

If you are not well within yourself, then how can you be well within a group? It is the individual who is the thread to this fabric of society. Your part to play is not one to be taken lightly. For yourself, you must follow the path that leads to your destiny, and for society you must leave something worthwhile behind.

Being one of a kind means you have something special to offer, something unique. Seek not to identify with others, but to stand out from the crowd. You are extraordinary. Why settle for an ordinary lifestyle, with an ordinary pay check, with ordinary results and people? Never stoop to suffice small minds but stand tall and rise to take charge of your life!

Time goes at a steady pace, second
to minutes to hours to days to
weeks. You will be surprised how
the years go by. If you stop or pause
or freeze, know that time will never
mimic your actions. Time is an ever-
going, sovereign entity which
governs your every movement. If it
is not contained or managed wisely,
then it is easily wasted and used for
matters which will not benefit you.

Discontinuation of progress is the
equivalent of giving up. It is the
equivalent of time and its cycles
getting a hold of you. However, since
time is cyclical, that simply means it
can be studied, and anything that
can be studied can be mastered.
Make a study of when you are
fruitful and when you are barren.

Rather than only feasting during the times you have plenty, learn to prepare yourself for the dry seasons to follow. Gluttony of success often leads to laziness. Likewise, starvation of success feeds mediocrity. It is the duty of the success-seeking individual to harness the power needed to overcome both laziness and mediocrity, and the level the playing field by being an active player.

What will you leave behind to say, "I was here on earth"? How will you sign your name? The value of your work is best summed up and greatest when you are no longer of this world. The treasure of words and books, creativity and creations, sports playing and record making, songs and songbooks, are available to us because others who are now dead and gone dared to leave something of value behind. It is your name that lives on after you. Rather, it is the value of your name. The character is behind the name; the products and services are behind the name; the awards and achievement are behind the name.

You have something one of a kind to present to the world. It is called your signature. It is what you are to be noted for. You must find your signature and release it. Free it so that you too can be free. Summon it so that your destiny can be summoned. Until you find your signature you cannot save yourself. Until you find your signature, you will not actualize your potential and realize your greatness.

New ideas, new ventures, new information and new hobbies are just are few of the things you should pursue. Become familiar with all corners of life – the good, the bad, the ups and the downs. Experience is one of the best learning methods, which is why you should want to do more and become more.

There is so much out there that you are ignorant of. Venture out to widen your sources of knowledge. Yes, it is not possible to know everything. However, it is possible to do as much as you can and know as much as you can. The more you search and find out is the more you grow, even more so, is the more you know.

Exploration is the search for the unknown. That is most likely the reason many fear new things, for the sake of the unknown. Fear should never be the reason you fail to try, yet in most instances it is. Overcome your fears by yearning for more. Be hungry for more and work towards more. It is safe to say that a sense of fulfilment comes with the garnering of newness.

It is one thing to be dipped in darkness, those times when everything is rolling down hill and progress is little to none. It is yet another thing to experience sunlight, a moment in your life when happiness and opportunities spring forth.

There are many fluctuations between those two episodes within a lifetime. How do you take control so that you can experience more happiness than despair? It takes a high degree of consciousness to master the art of seeing the best in tough times. It takes practice. It takes choice. You can't be so "high" in your high moments that you forget that something will come along to tilt your even scale.

When you know that, then you can prepare yourself and are likely to better adjust yourself. Likewise, you cannot be so "low" in your low moments that you become oblivious to that little bit of light shining in. In the same way, you are to be prepared for new opportunities. There is a continuous cycle of dawn and dusk, great periods and terrible periods. You have no control over the flow of the cycle, however, you do have control over your attitude. Learn to appreciate that bit of light that is ever present in your darkest moments.

An opportunity serves as both an entrance into the new life you desire and an exit from the unsatisfactory one. Do not expect the open doors of opportunity to remain so just for your benefit. You have to grab the chances while you can and as fast as you can.

What you take a minute to think about can be taken away in seconds by the man who yearns more for success. Note however, that some traps are disguised as opportunities. Be quick to evaluate and quick to decide.

You do not want to find yourself in a situation that hurts you or your character in any way. If you are struggling and looking for a way out, then an open door is your answer. This may come in the form of an opportunity, an idea, or even a talent. The open door may just be in the power of your choice.

It is your decision to say that you have had enough...that you have wallowed in hopelessness enough. Get up, get going, and walk proudly through your open door. What lies on the other side is what you deserve, is everything you have imagined, hoped for, and dreamed of. It takes decisions to change your life. To sit and hope that everything will get better is only part of the formula. The rest is based on your decisions and your actions as a result of what you hope for.

Can you see yourself having everything you have ever desired? Where do you see yourself a month from now, a year from now or a decade from now? Do you see things changing for you? The routine that you submit yourself to might just well be keeping you from the future you deserve.

Shake things up a bit. Trade in your comfort for profitability. Lack of sleep, entertainment, friendly gatherings and relaxation are but a few of the things that you are likely to give up for the focus on what is ahead of you. The permanence of your future is sure. Do you want to be permanently free and happy, or permanently enslaved and miserable?

For the permanence of a happy future, temporarily neglect the discomfort that accompanies working on your dreams. If what you see in the future is not to your liking, then you can change it by doing something about it right now.

That comes with changing up your regular lifestyle and doing some out of the norm, extraordinary things. Don't you want to be able to say "I love the view" when scoping out your future? Get to work.

As you are building and creating, or once you have built and created, outside forces in many forms will come to destroy what you worked so hard for. It is within your own best interest that you pay close attention to the people you bring in your circle, the places you go, the things you say, and the things you do. Sometimes just affiliating with the wrong persons can cause trouble. Have an all-round surveillance of your empire.

This means making note of everything and everyone that operates within, throughout and outside of it. Note attitudes, actions, words, functionality and genuineness. If anything or anyone seems to be the least bit out of place, do not hesitate to get the problem fixed or get rid of what's causing the problem. The slightest mishap can escalate to the point where it causes destruction.

You may find a plunge in your finances, your health, your spirituality, your relationships and so much more by simply making a bad decision or compromising for the sake of someone else. Protect and keep both eyes on what you have birthed.

One major red flag is when you are thrown off balance or feel off balance. It is a sign that you have taken the wrong route. You have an internal map, which guides you to your dream destination. You also have an internal alarm which goes off when you travel the wrong way. Follow your instinct, it is yet another internal tool to guide you.

Everything you need to reach success is within you. Life throws a break every now and again in the form of warnings. It is when you ignore those warnings that failure happens over and over again. Failure should not be feared but rather failure to learn from a failure. Do not focus on what you did wrong but what you can do right the next time around.

Appreciate your failures as they act as buffers to possible annihilation of your dreams. They are there to keep you centered. Imagine yourself drifting from your dreams only to be pushed back in line by a failure. They prevent your total derailment and are present all around to keep you aligned. "BE CAREFUL DANGER TO YOUR DREAMS AHEAD" is what all red flags warn. Heed to warning.

Whomsoever you portray yourself to be should be who you are, or who you hope to be. A life of lies both to yourself and others is sure to backfire. People can sense sincerity and genuineness. Likewise, they can sense pretentiousness. Wear your true self on your sleeve, show your true personality.

At times, one can be so layered that when the layers are peeled away, it comes as a surprise to those around to see who you really are. Be comfortable with yourself enough to be open around others. No one likes a liar or a deceptive individual.

Build trust and not caution with others. Your reputation is dependent on your level of trustworthiness. When you present yourself to the world, you want to be viewed as someone of value. People accept value and virtue over pretense and vices. The truth has a funny way of finding light. Honesty is your best bet at winning over your fans or prospects or buyers of your services. When it is hardest to do is when you must choose to be honest.

Constantly ask yourself, "How can I be better?" You want to be overflowing with so much value that success comes running at your feet. Your mindset has just about everything to do with where you are and what you have gotten from life. Are you a positive or negative thinker? Are you conscious of your success? How about your money making? Believe it or not, the majority of people don't prioritize their success, they only speak of it. They aren't working on their dreams, are not working on themselves, and are definitely not researching possible sources of money and success.

They have limited themselves to their regular jobs and careers, only to the detriment of their dreams. That is exactly why dreams die. When the mind is not set on achieving goals and doing more, it is reduced to a state of mediocrity. You will not and cannot change until your way of thinking has changed. Your life will not change until you make a full three hundred and sixty degree turn around in your mind. It is a fight, but you must first master yourself before you can master success. Start a revolution in your mind. Go against the system you are set to. See what difference it can make in your journey and future.

Be a source of encouragement. Why, with so many people in it, can the world be such a lonely place? Everyone is about their own business. No time to stop and ask, "How is your day today?" The hustle and bustle of life is all around. We are all so focused on getting where we need to go, that we forget about neighborly love. Sometimes all another needs is a good word.

A little tap on the shoulder to say, "Hey, everything will be okay." It's so easy to envelope ourselves with work and school, and everything outside of ourselves, that we lose ourselves. We lose the importance of ourselves. Each man carries the role to be a brother's or a sister's keeper. Be a vessel which pours out inspiration and motivation. It could be in the form of a smile, or a good word or a helpful hand. Be an example of what it means to do your best and be your best. Let them see your perseverance. Let them see your determination. Let them see you hard at work. When they see your accumulation of riches and fortunes, they will know it is not by luck but rather by effort and good will.

Do not chase riches by selling your time for the accumulation of it. This will only push you further away from what you are destined to be in life. You can never have more time, but you can however, get the most out of each second, minute, and hour.

By adding value to your time, then
money, if that's your aim, will flow
in. How do you add value to your
time? By beginning to be more than
you are. Then and only then, will
the fortune you and every being is
destined to have, be in your
possession. You can always have
more money, but you can never have
more time. So what do you deem
more valuable, the former or the
latter? Time my friend, is the
essence of life. Harness it and you
will be happy. Freedom of time is
the dream of most men. That's why
we take vacations which we feel give
us more time, and complain of work
which steals our time. Imagine a life
where every day feels like a
vacation. The only way to
accomplish this is by taking full
control of our time and hence feel
more fulfilled and happy.

Many make the mistake of blaming poverty solely on the lack of money. Little do they know that it is ignorance which breeds the lack thereof. Do not count yourself in the lot. The more you know, the more valuable you become.

The more valuable you become, the more you can make for your time. Until you acquire new knowledge, you will never know what pivotal information you are insufficient in. That might just be the knowledge or skill to help mold the ideas which will take you closer to your destiny, if not directly to it. Be a gatherer of information. Read the necessary books, research as much as possible, learn from the mistakes and experiences of others, and study your own experiences. Life is one big experiment. Draw evidence from all sources, the good and the bad, and be sure to observe. That way, you will prove right and accurate, the hypothesis that one can mold and create a life that was once just a mere idea.

Engage in activities and practice behaviors that will make you happy. Surround yourself with positive, uplifting individuals. It won't be too long that their attitude will influence you. Wake up with a smile on your face, even if it's the start of the work week. Bring that fire from the weekend into your weekdays.

Your face should not reflect your problems. Many would say walk it off, but it's so much easier to laugh it off. Laughter brings healing in many forms. It is a remedy for negatives such as anger, sadness, loneliness, depression, and anxiety. Anything that takes away from your happiness is a negative. Rid yourself of them. Happiness, is a choice. It is the habit you want to form. It is not something that will come when you have the perfect car, or the perfect job, or the perfect house, or the perfect amount of money. Stop waiting for the perfect time to be happy. While doing so, you are only starving your soul – the center of your being. The time is now. Feel the joy of the moment. Things might not be all well but you have life and that's something to smile about, so smile.

You are the keeper, the owner of your destiny. It is not until you voice that it is under your rule and power that you breathe life into you it. Declaration of your destiny is a declaration of self, your declaration of purpose.

When you know what you were made for, then acting in part becomes less confusing and more certain. It is certainty in who you are and what you are capable of. It is a point where you are no longer afraid of your light or to shine it blindingly among others. That leap of faith is promising now. That act of valor to self no longer seems selfish in your eyes but self-less.

For in declaring your destiny, you are adding worth to the world. You are adding yourself as a great figure, whether recognized or unsung. You are adding wealth by grasping your waiting fortune. You have seen the summit and its promise has you sprinting up the mountain. It is the act of a champion to declare their destiny.

22126201R00063

Made in the USA
Columbia, SC
23 July 2018